This book belongs to:

Text copyright © 2021 Caterpillar Books Ltd.
Cover art and interior illustrations copyright © 2021 by WeDoo Studio
All rights reserved. Published in the United States by The Reading House,
an imprint of Random House Children's Books, a division of Penguin
Random House LLC, New York. The Reading House and the colophon
are registered trademarks of Penguin Random House LLC.
rhcbooks.com
Educators and librarians, for a variety of teaching tools,
visit us at RHTeachersLibrarians.com
ISBN: 978-0-59345-042-0
Printed in China
10 9 8 7 6 5 4 3 2 1
First North American Edition
CPB/1800/1774/0221

Random House Children's Books supports the
First Amendment and celebrates the right to read.

Penguin Random House LLC supports copyright.
Copyright fuels creativity, encourages diverse voices, promotes
free speech, and creates a vibrant culture. Thank you for buying an
authorized edition of this book and for complying with copyright laws
by not reproducing, scanning, or distributing any part in any form
without permission. You are supporting writers and allowing
Penguin Random House to publish books for every reader.

My First Learning Skills

Contents

Welcome to The Reading House   5

Hints and Tips for Parents and Guardians   6

Pencil Control   8

Colors   12

Shapes   14

Alphabet   16

Numbers and Early Math   38

Sorting and Classifying   56

Opposites   66

Everyday Skills   68

Emotions and Senses   70

Basic Vocabulary   72

Answers   76

Certificate   79

Welcome to The Reading House

Marla Conn, MS. Ed., is a reading and literacy specialist with a Master of Science in Elementary Education and Reading and 15 years' experience as a teacher in New York public schools.

During my years as a teacher, literacy specialist, and Educational Consultant, I have worked with hundreds of children and have a deep understanding of how the right books and instructional materials can provide rich, meaningful experiences that build a strong foundation for learning.

The Reading House was created out of the need for a comprehensive and systematic educational tool, combining dependable strategies that have been proven to motivate, educate, and spark the process of learning, using an innovative storybook, character-based approach.

What began as a leveled learn-to-read scheme has grown into an entire educational universe, with learning materials to cover all aspects of early learning, in a variety of educational formats. Each book in the series has been carefully devised and designed to inspire and encourage young learners, and adheres to the core principles and key building blocks of early learning.

The Reading House is one-of-a-kind; an inviting, accessible educational space where children can learn and grow. With its engaging cast of characters, bright and playful illustrations, and consistent setting, The Reading House is a world that early learners will love, and to which they will want to return, again and again.

I am so excited for children to get their hands on these books, and to watch the lightbulb switch on!

Happy Reading!
Marla Conn

Hints and Tips for Parents and Guardians

My First Learning Skills is designed to improve confidence and ability in a range of early learning concepts for pre-kindergarten learners. Designed to be as enjoyable as it is educational, little learners are joined on their journey by the fantastically fun cast of The Reading House.

From basic pencil control through the alphabet, number order through early math, and everything in between—including shapes, colors, patterns, emotions and everyday skills—this workbook is the perfect introduction to the most important basics, and a launchpad for learning.

As you work through this workbook with your little one, talk through activities clearly and patiently, encourage and ask questions, and allow breaks as necessary.

Before embarking on the learning journey, there are a few hints and tips parents and guardians should bear in mind.

 HELP:

As you progress through the workbook with your child, help them by reading instructions aloud and explaining activities further.

 COMMON STROKES:

The workbook begins with an introduction to pre-writing skills and common pencil strokes. It is important to start with these activities, as the strokes practiced here form the basis of the correct formulation of shapes, letters and numbers, which are covered in detail in the remainder of the workbook.

 MANIPULATIVES:

When it comes to numbers, many children will benefit from seeing and handling physical objects, or manipulatives (items such as buttons or blocks) to help them in the process of counting.

 ANSWERS:

Refer to the answers section at the back of the workbook once your child has completed an activity. Ensure they fully comprehend the concept presented before moving on to the next activity.

⭐ **WRITING INSTRUMENT AND GRASP:**

Your child will probably already be familiar with holding a crayon, and a short crayon is a perfectly acceptable beginner writing instrument. As their hand muscles and fine motor skills develop, you should encourage your child to use a short pencil, and later, at around age four, a standard-sized pencil.

You should demonstrate ideal pencil grasp to your child, per the following steps:

We love learning in **Happy Town!**

- Hold the pencil between thumb and index finger, with index finger on top.

- Rest the pencil on the middle finger.

- Rest the side of the hand comfortably on the table.

⭐ **FORMATION:**

This workbook uses a system of dots and numbered arrows to demonstrate the correct formation of characters.

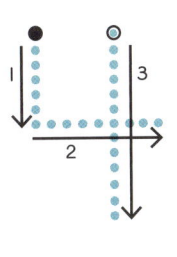

- The black dot indicates the starting point for the pencil.

- → The arrows show the direction of pencil movement, and should be followed in numerical order.

- This additional dot indicates that the pencil should leave the page to make a separate stroke.

⭐ **WRITING LINES:**

This workbook uses writing lines consisting of three lines with a dotted center to encourage proper character formation.

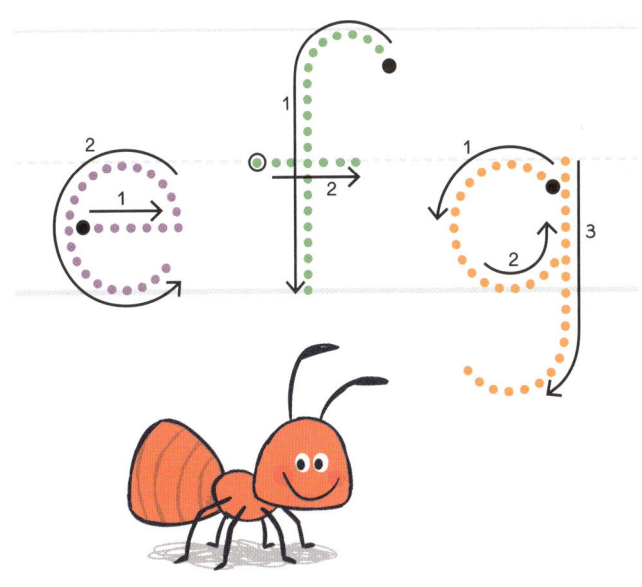

7

PENCIL CONTROL

Pencil Practice

Trace carefully along the **dotted** lines with your pencil. Start on the **black dot** and follow the **arrows**.

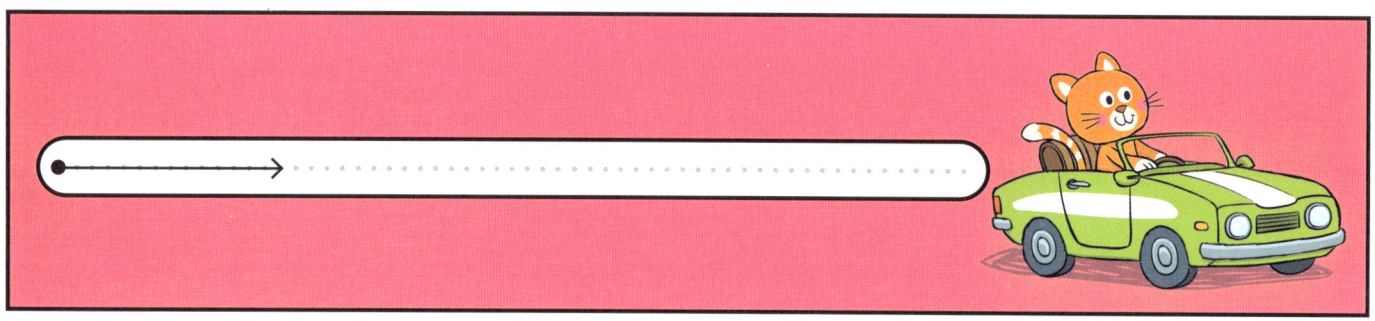

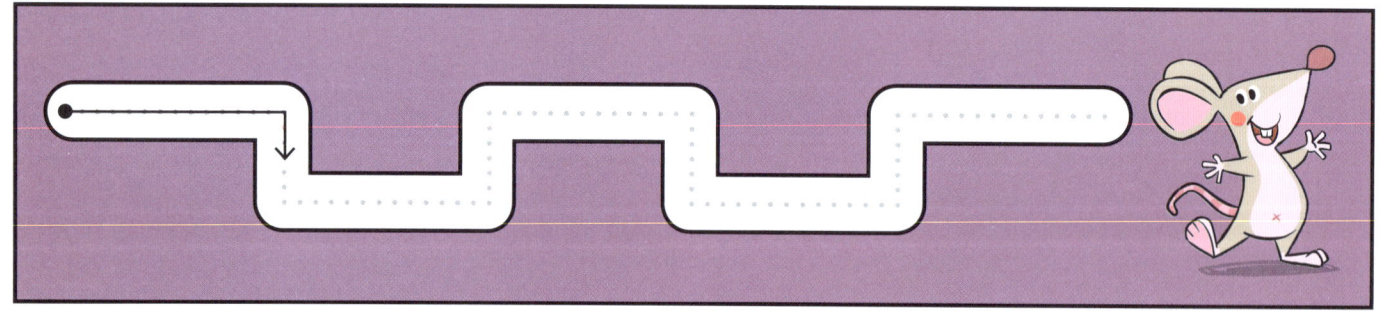

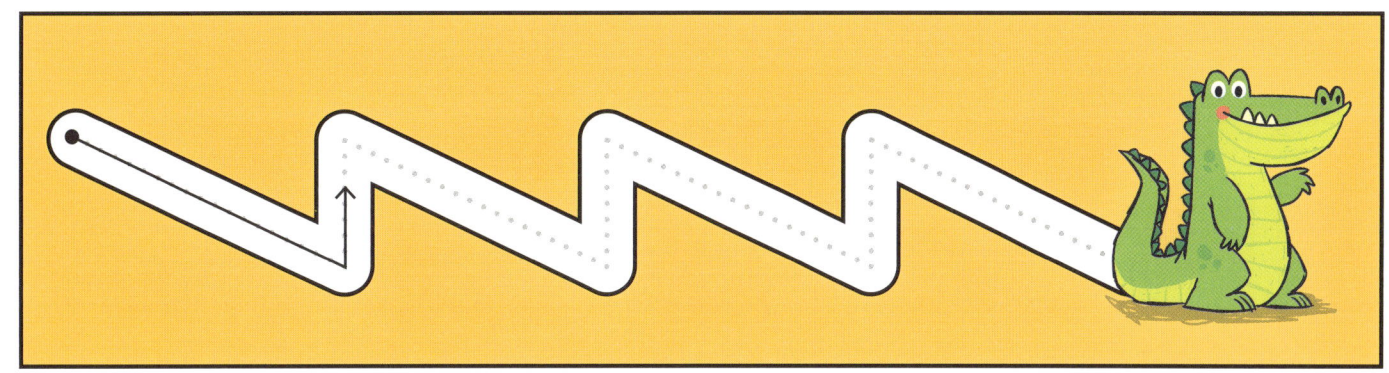

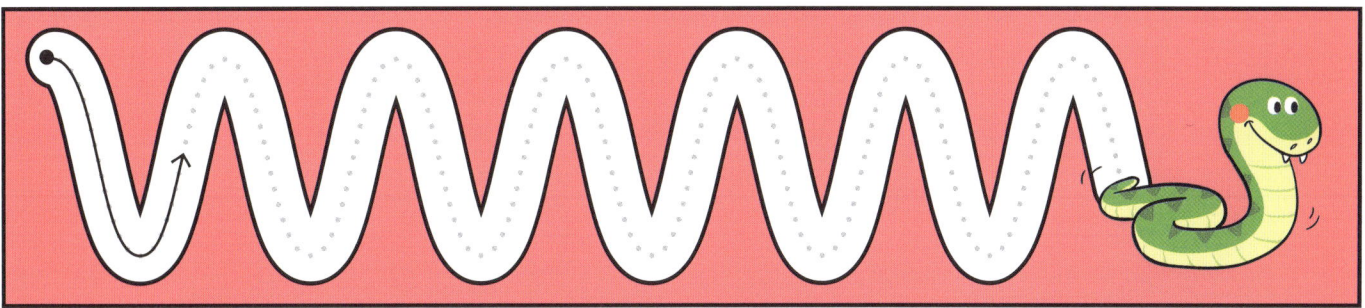
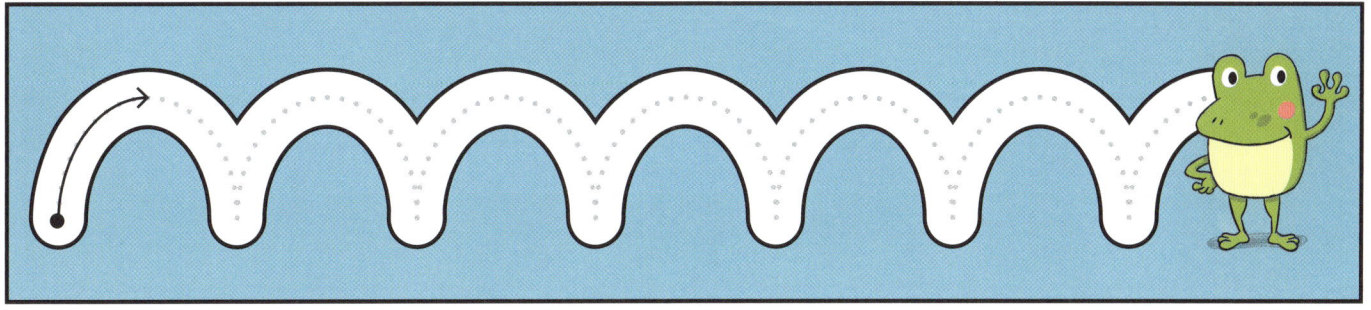

PENCIL CONTROL

Road to Happy Town

It's busy in **Happy Town**! Follow the road with your pencil, keeping the lines nice and straight.

Busy Bees

Bee and friends are **busy** at work!
Trace the curly path to the flower.

Colors

Draw lines to match the **colors** to their words in each activity. Say the words out loud.

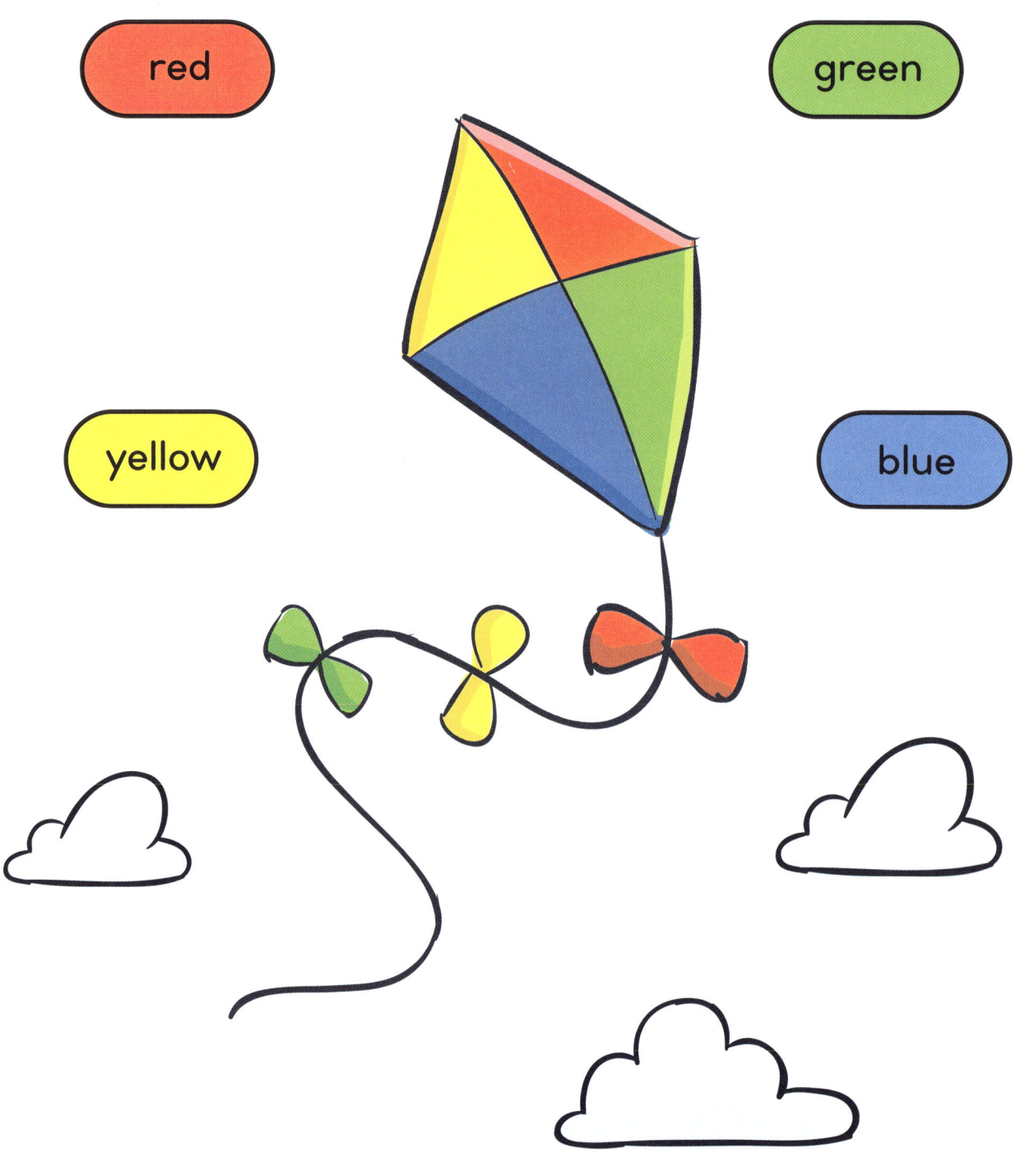

red

blue

pink

orange

purple

green

yellow

brown

SHAPES

Tracing Shapes

Start on the **black dot** and follow the **arrows** to trace each **shape**. When you have finished, color them in!

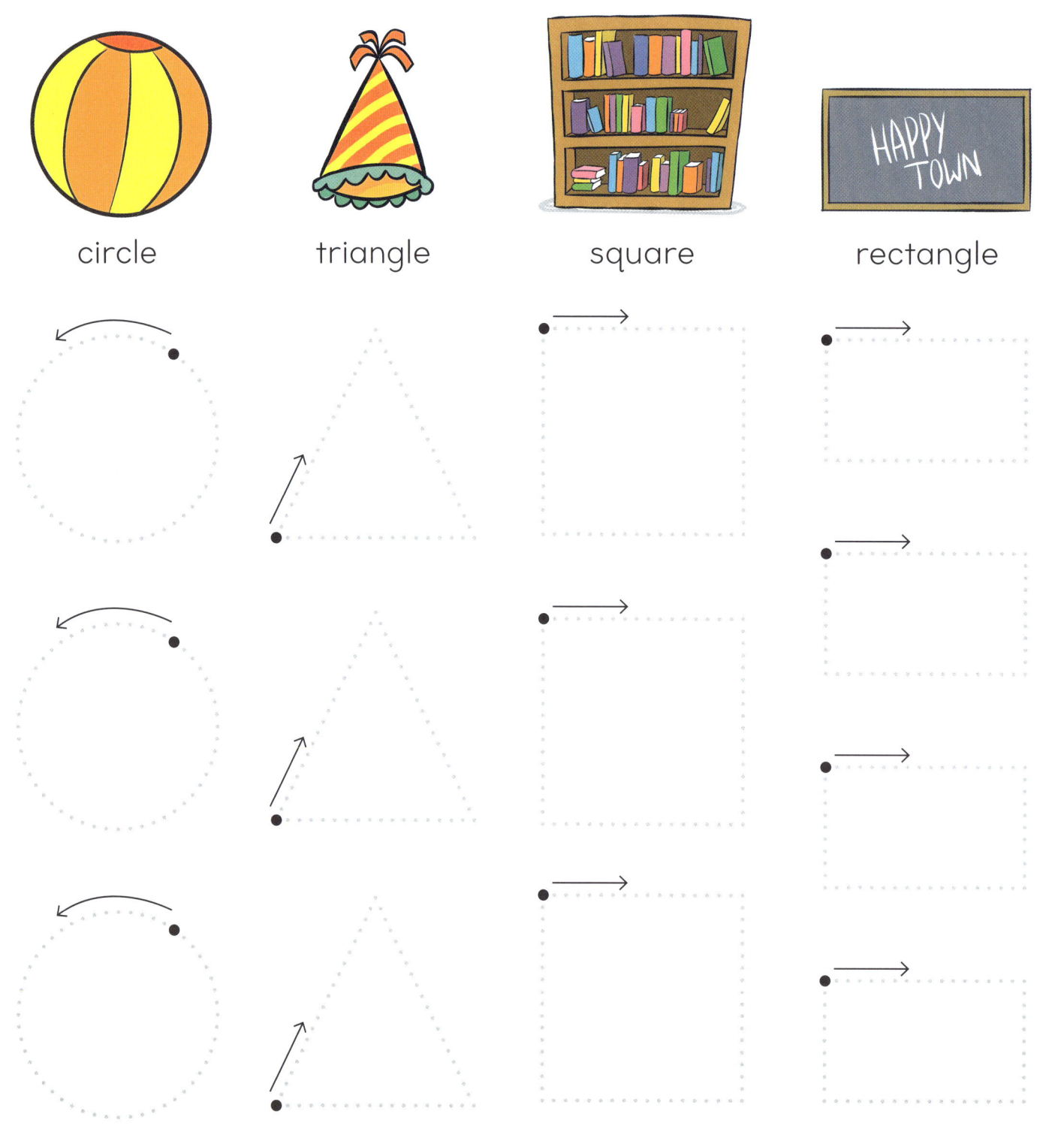

Color the Shape

Color the **shapes** in the colors indicated.

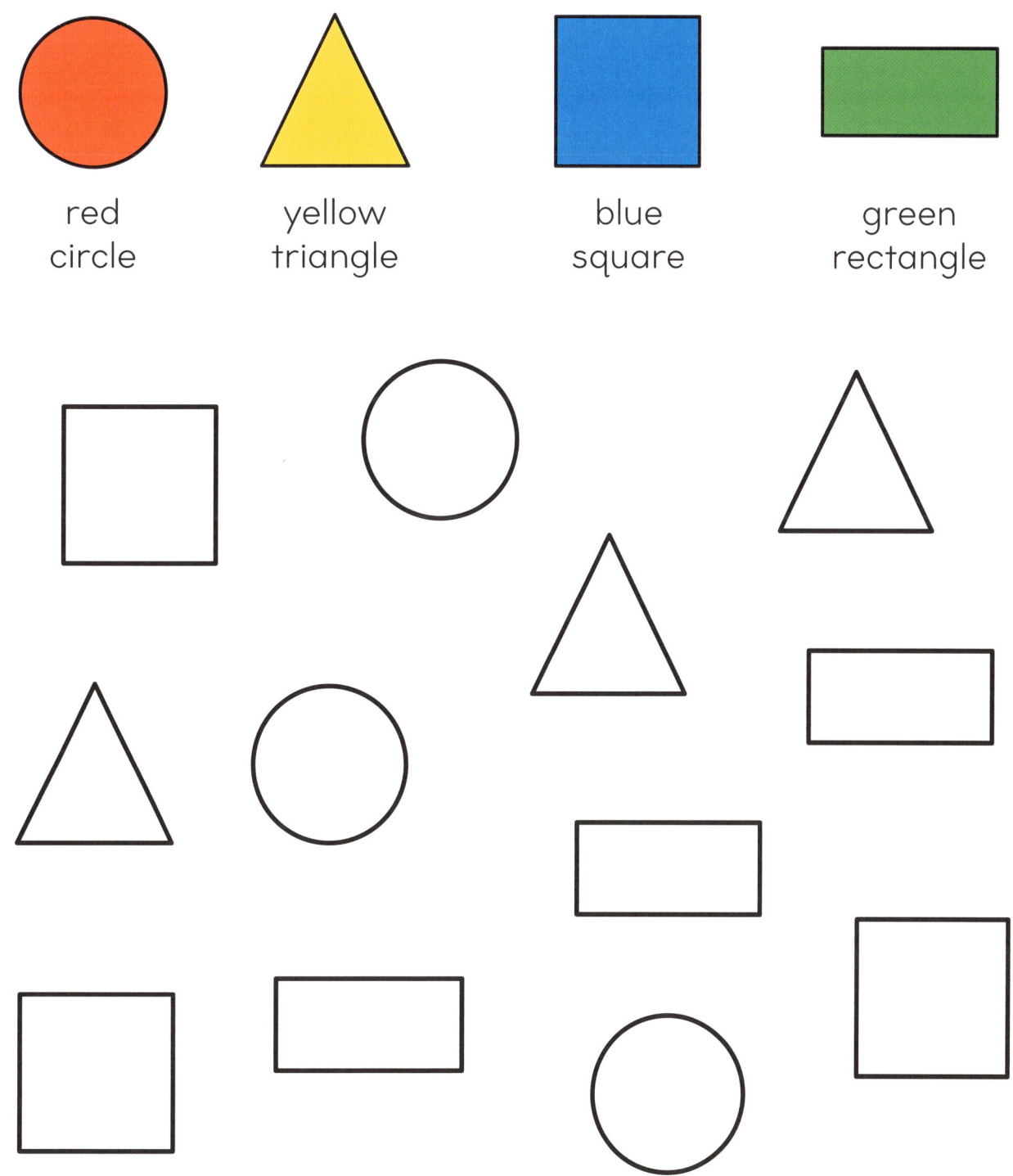

ALPHABET

Learning Aa to Zz

Trace the letters with your **finger**. Start on the **black dot** and follow the **arrows** in the correct order. Say the **sound** of the letter as you move your finger.

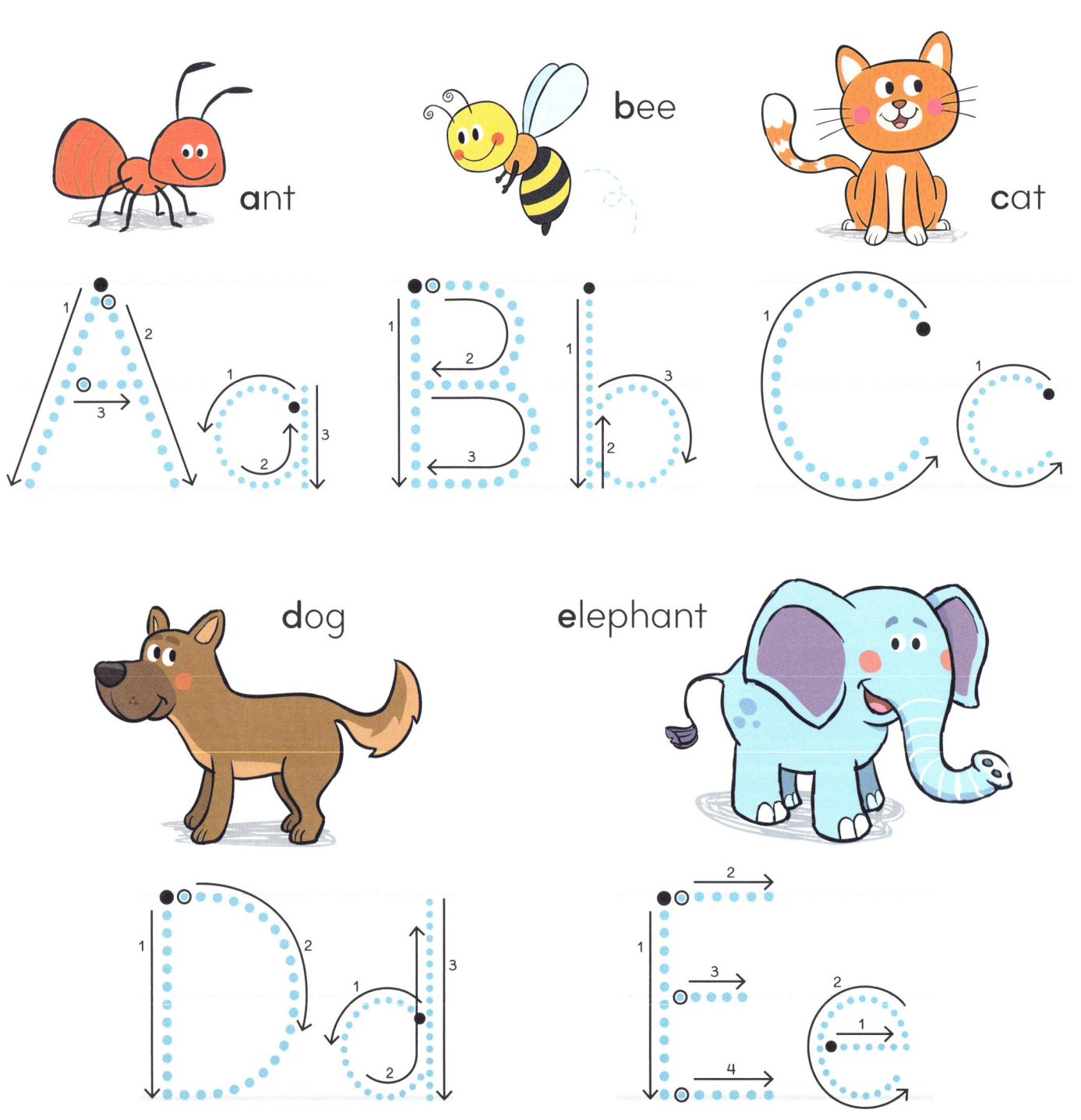

ant bee cat

dog elephant

16

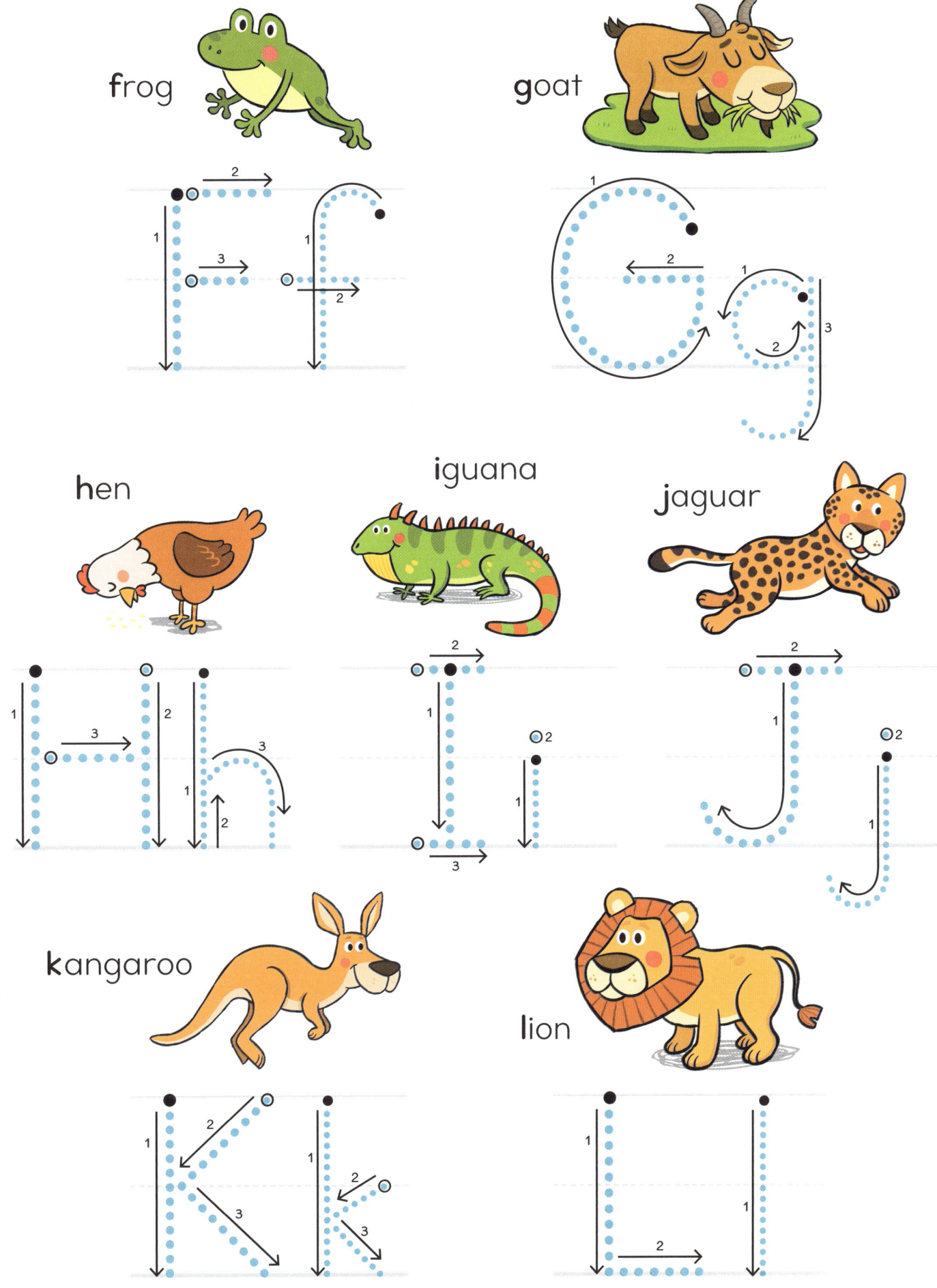

ALPHABET

18

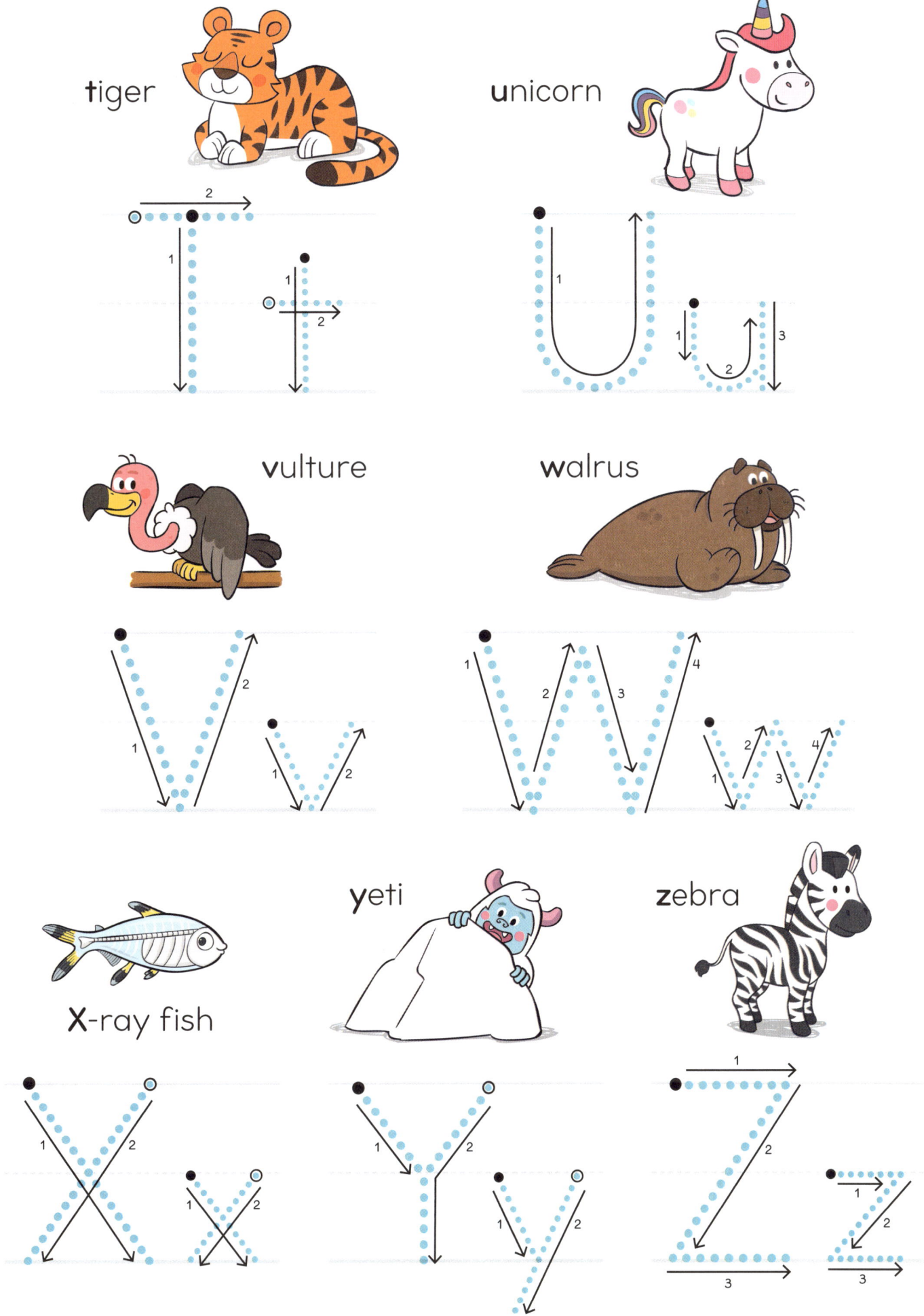

ALPHABET

Tracing Aa to Zz

Now use a **pencil** to trace all the letters.

Aa Bb Cc

Dd Ee Ff

Gg Hh Ii

Jj Kk Ll

ALPHABET

Uppercase and Lowercase Letters

Match the **uppercase** and **lowercase** letters.

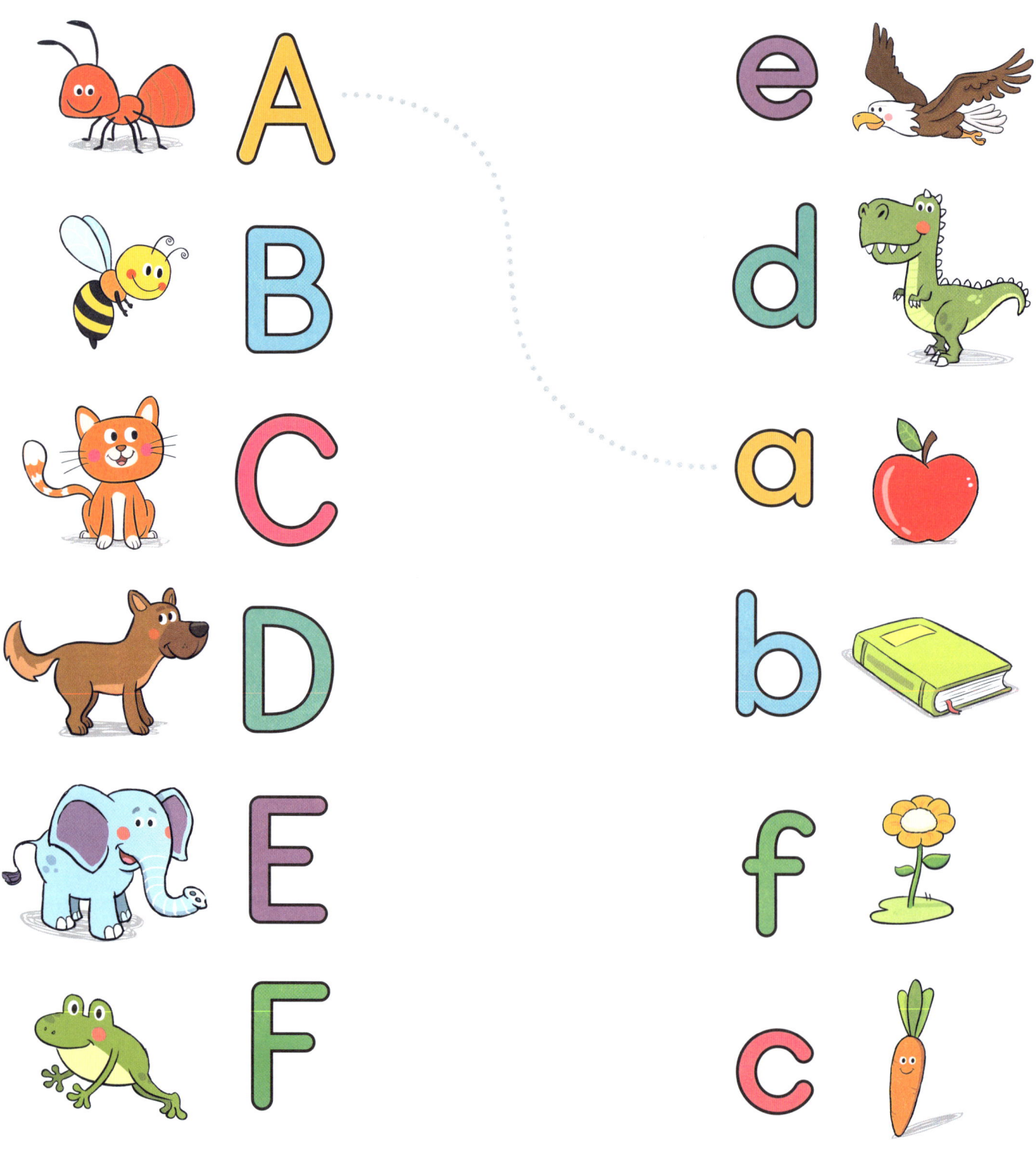

ALPHABET

N

O

P

Q

R

S

q

s

n

o

p

r

24

ALPHABET

Alphabet Match

With your pencil, trace the lines from the **letters** to the pictures.

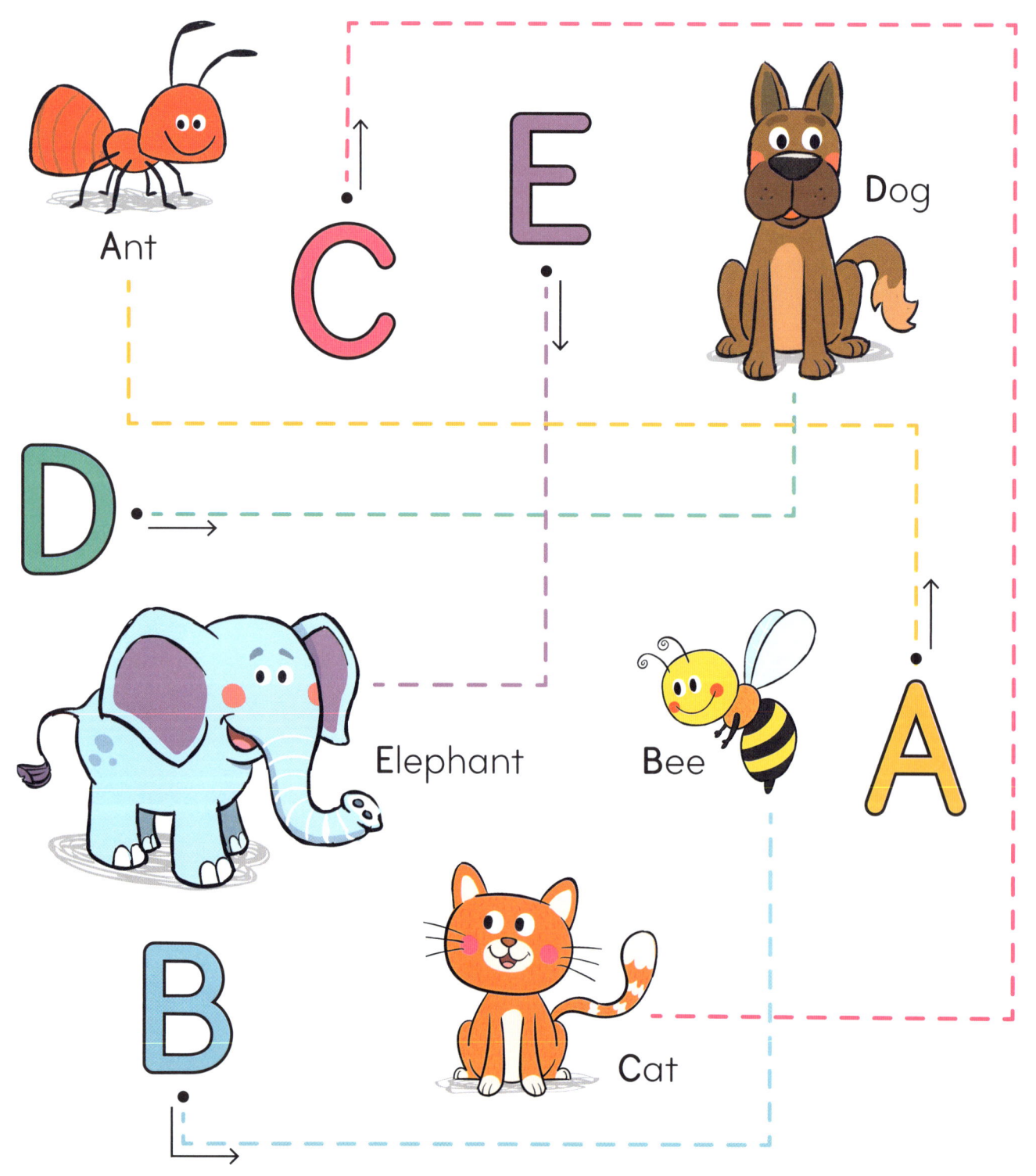

ALPHABET

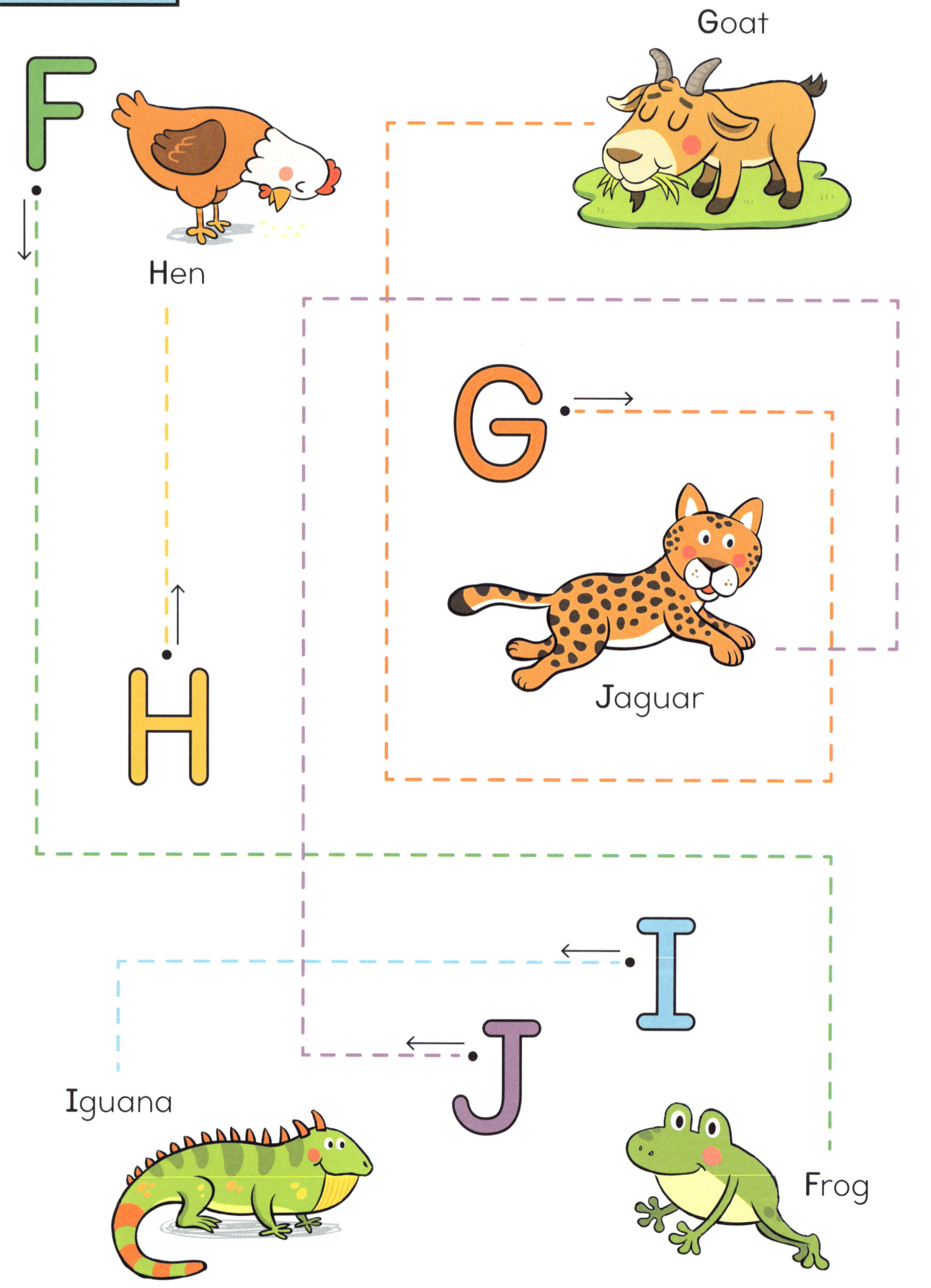

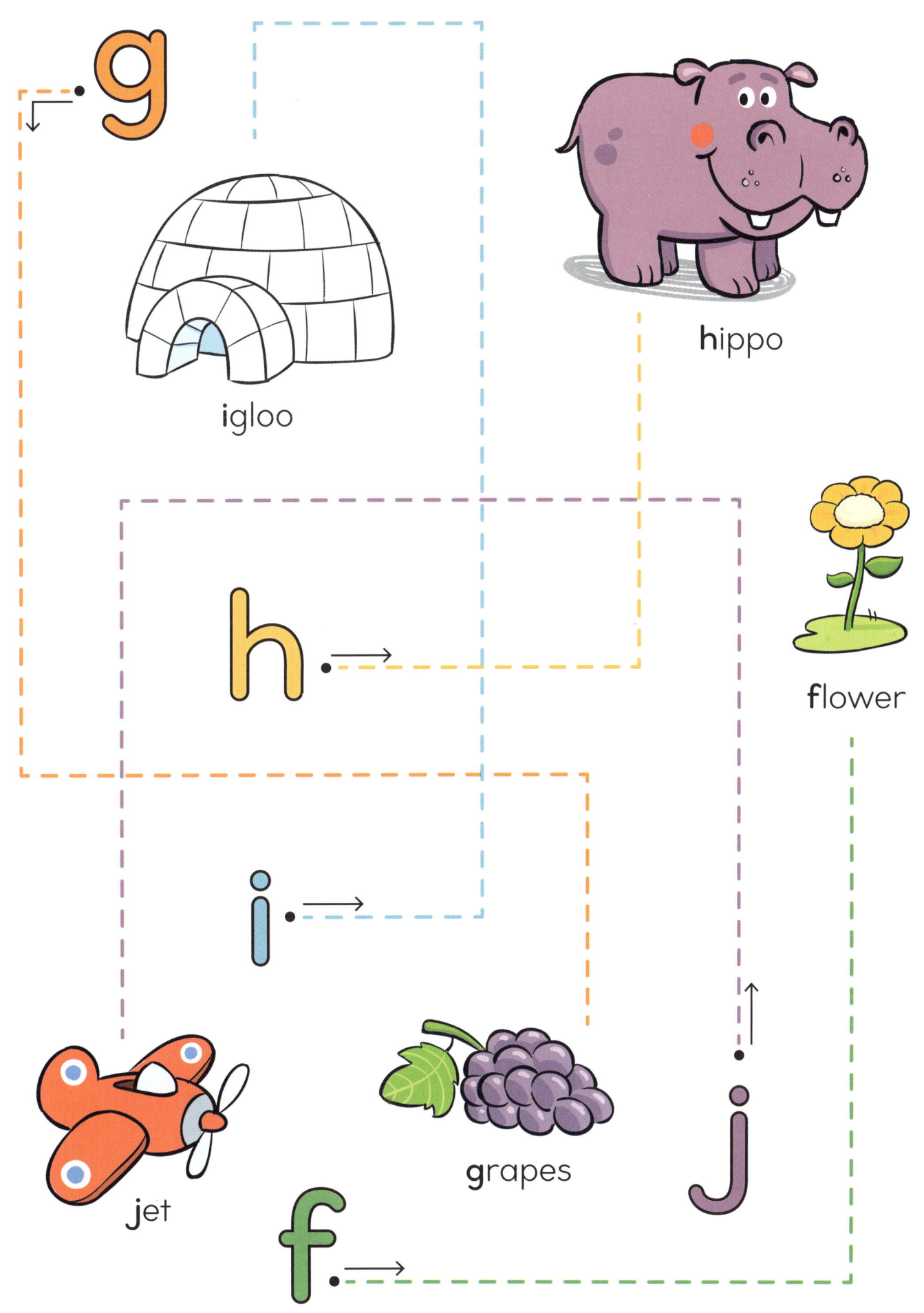

ALPHABET

30

ALPHABET

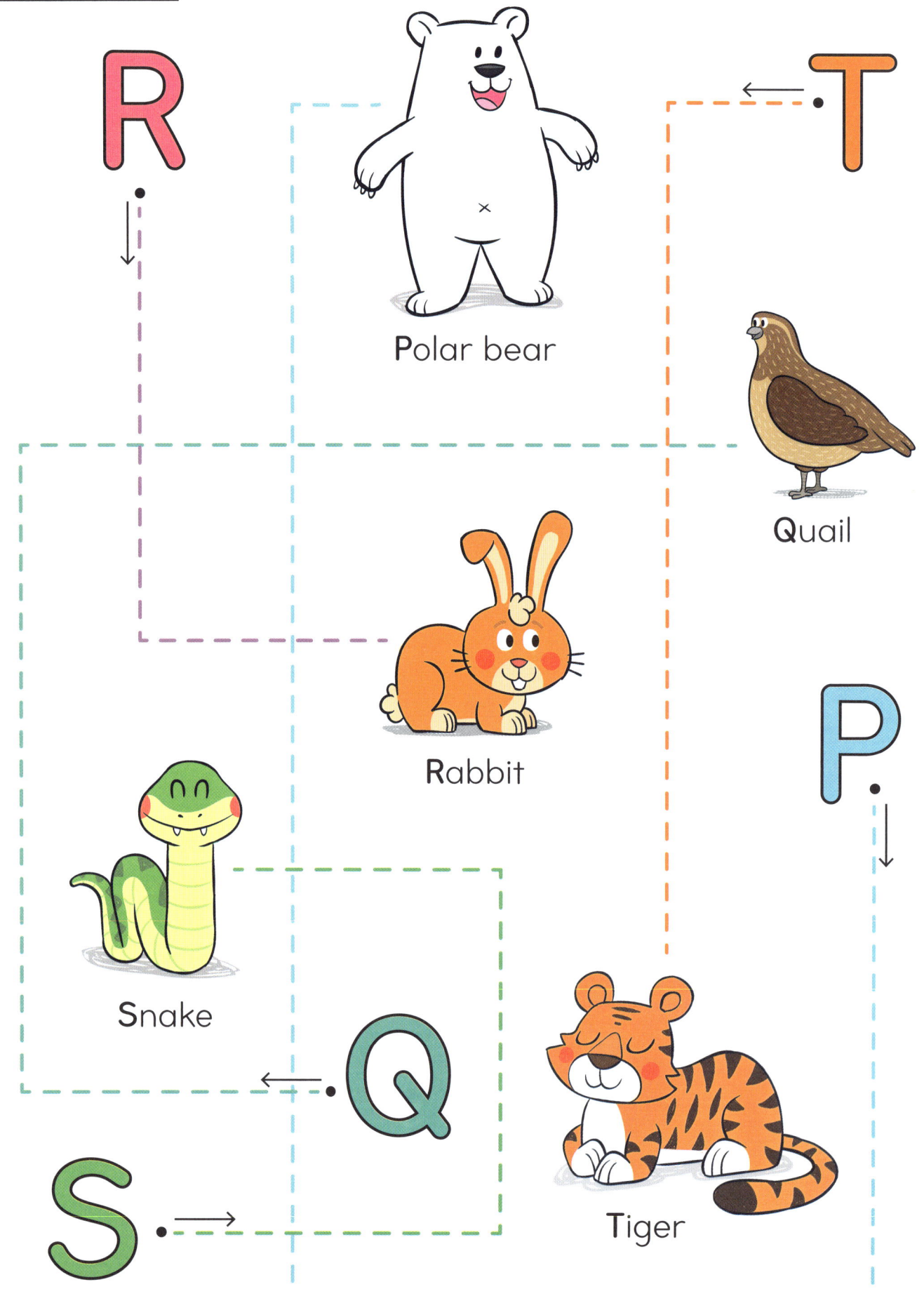

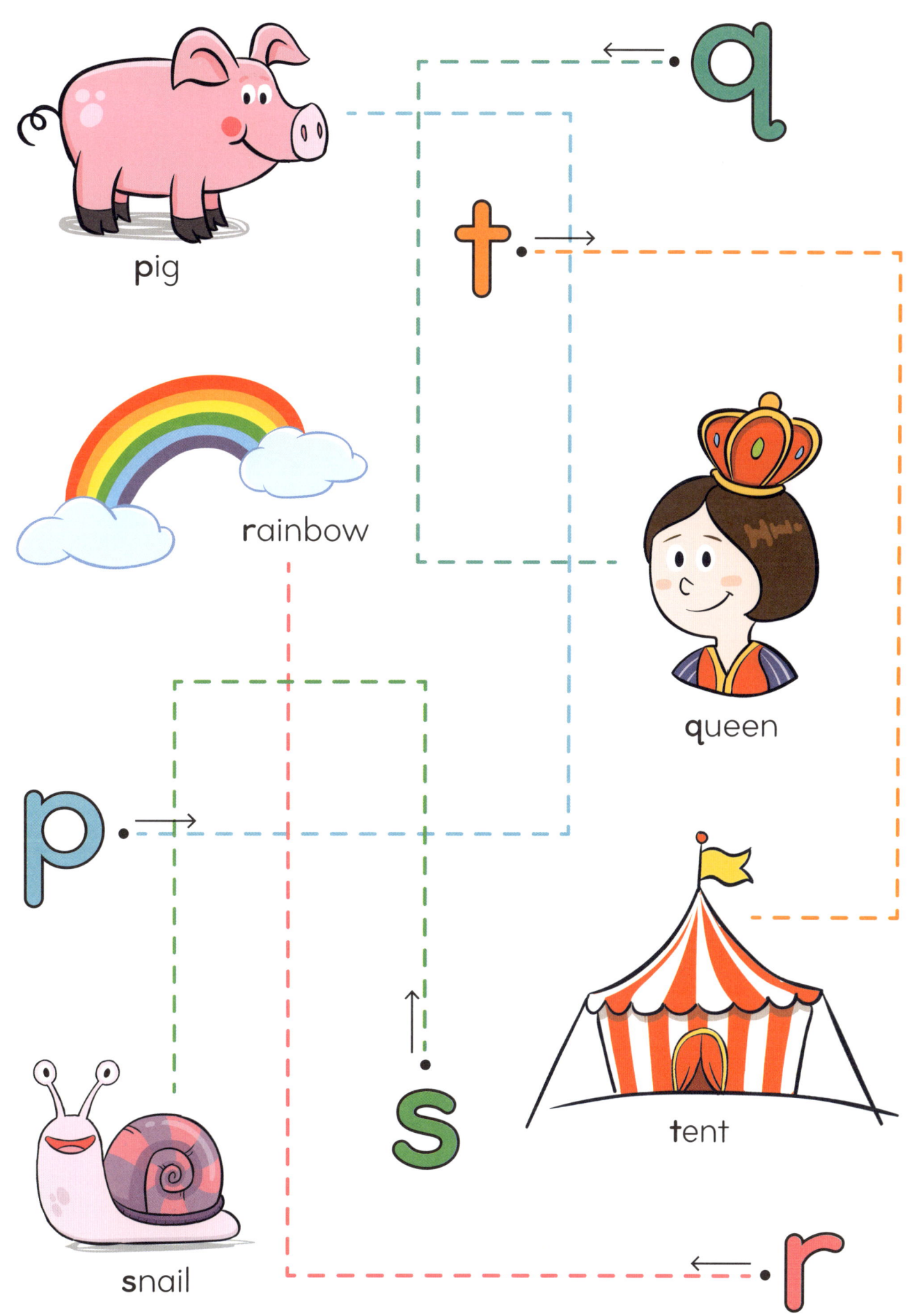

ALPHABET

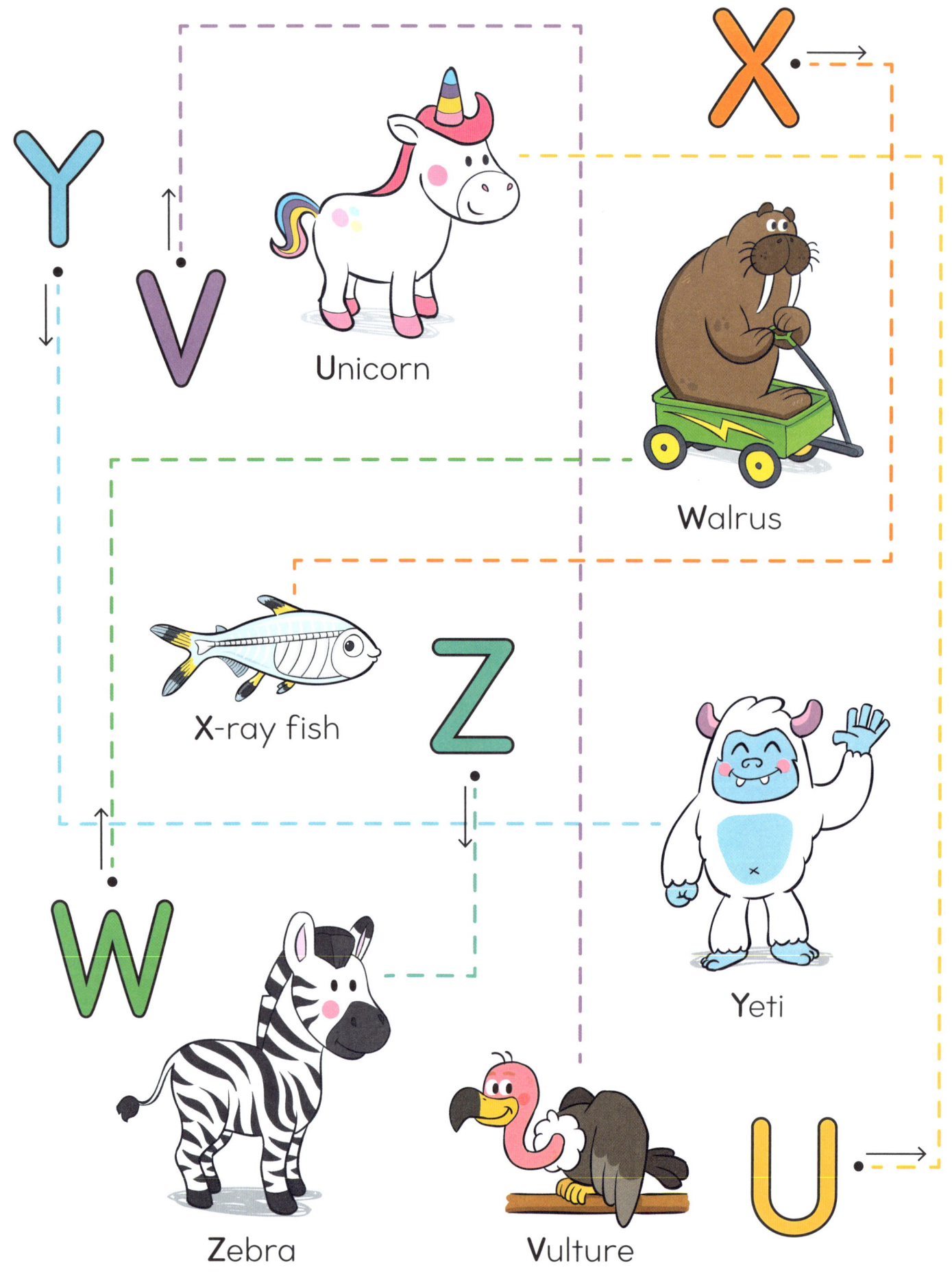

34

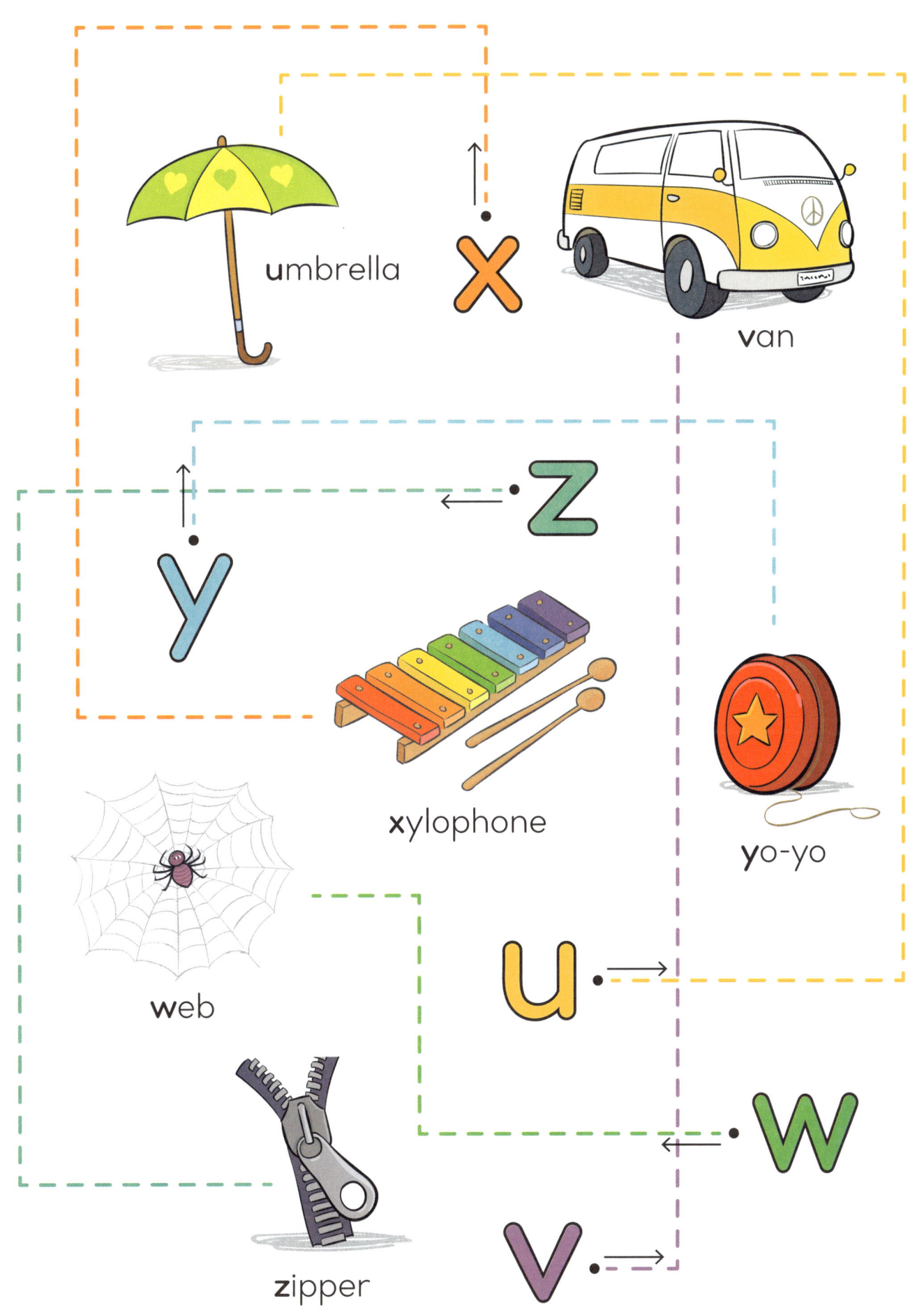

ALPHABET

Yeti's Alphabet Maze

Help **Yeti** through the maze by tracing a line from **A** to **Z** in the correct order.

Ant-astic Alphabet

Help **Ant** find a friend at the other side of the maze by tracing a line from **a** to **z**.

NUMBERS AND EARLY MATH

0, Zero

Trace the number 0.

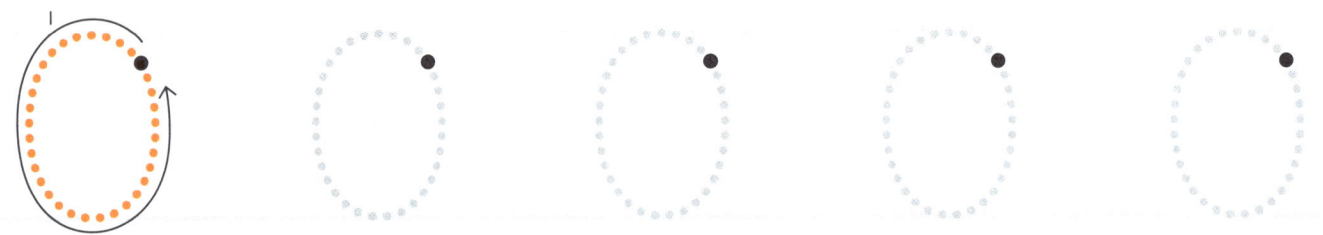

Circle all the 0s you can see.

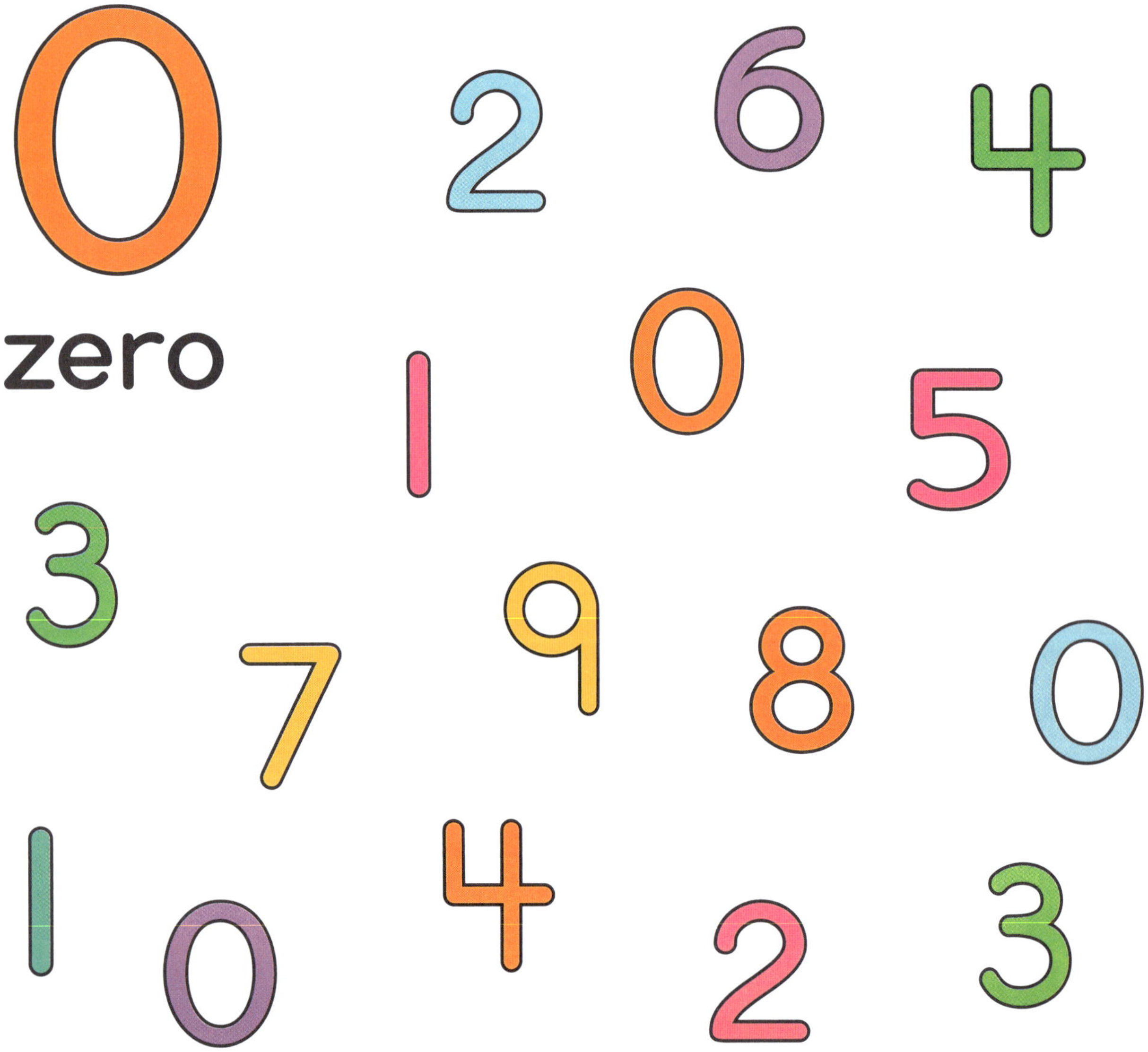

zero

1, One

Trace the number 1.

Color in 1 of the shapes with your favorite color!

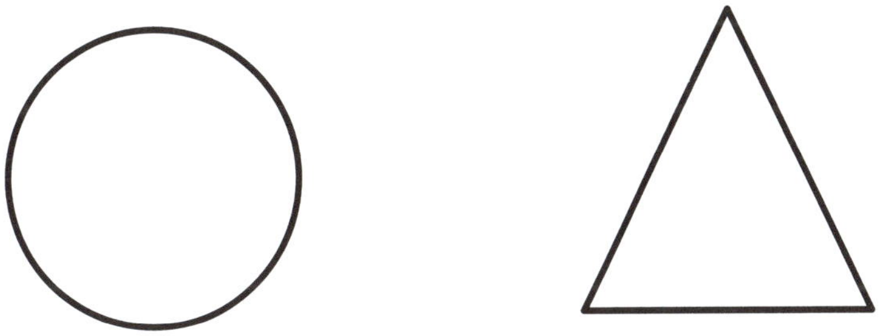

one

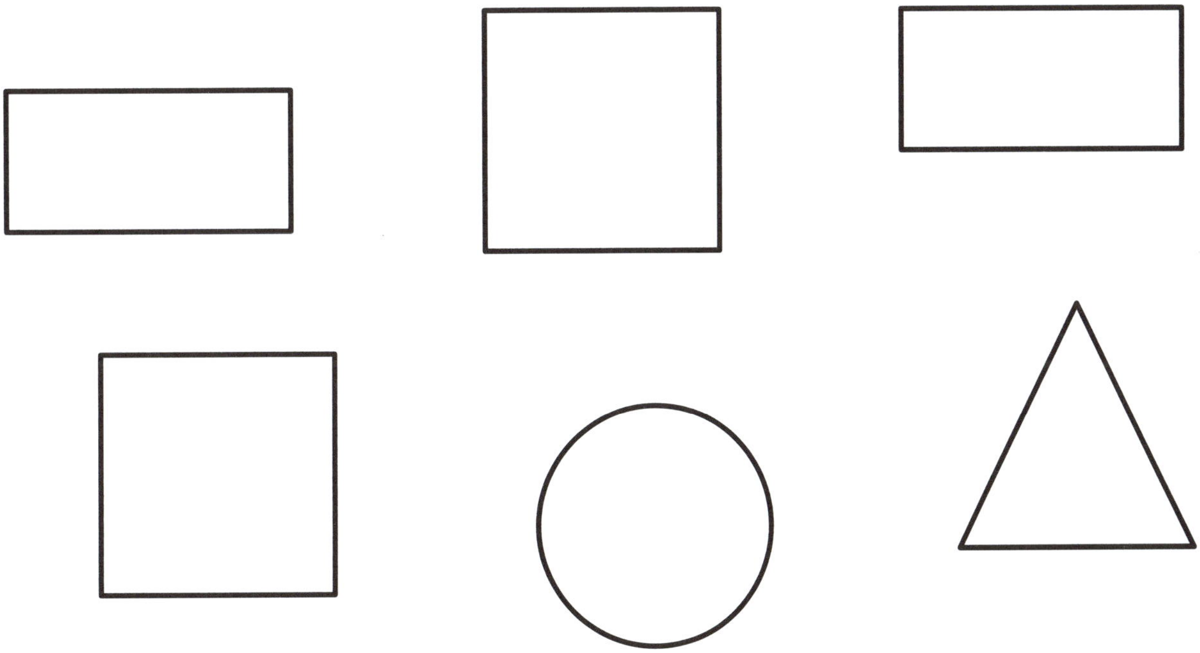

NUMBERS AND EARLY MATH

2, Two

Trace the number 2.

Draw lines from the number 2 to the groups of 2.

2 two

3, Three

Trace the number 3.

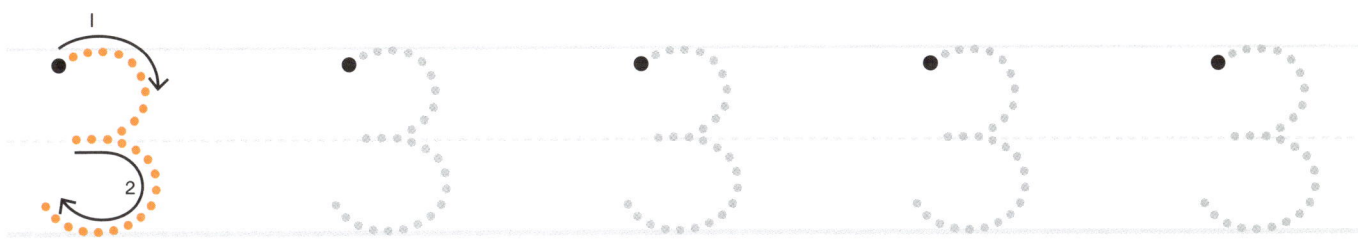

Circle **3** apples.

3
three

NUMBERS AND EARLY MATH

4, Four

Trace the number 4.

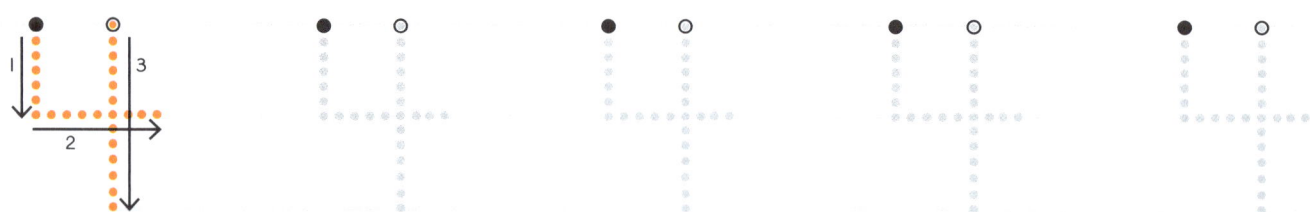

Circle the character with 4 legs.

4
four

Worms don't need legs to move!

5, Five

Trace the number **5**.

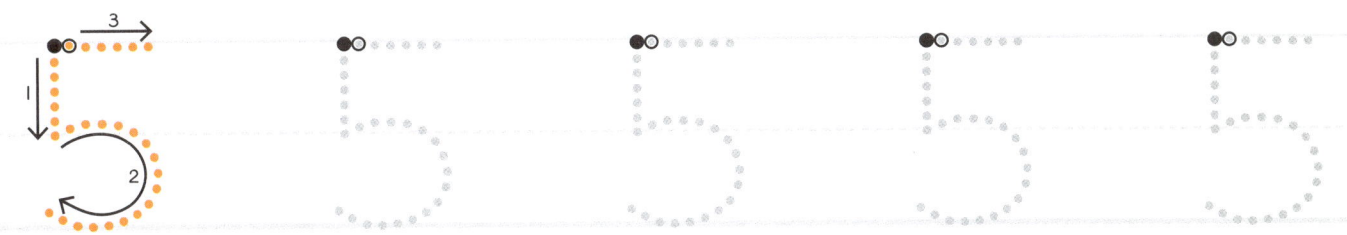

Color the **5** balls in the colors indicated below.

5
five

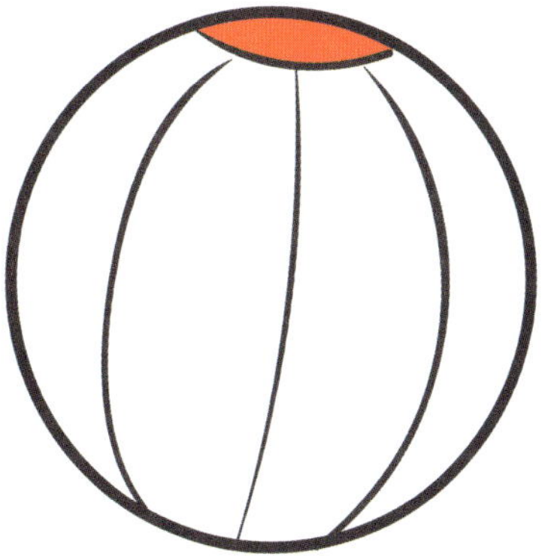

Color the ball **blue**.

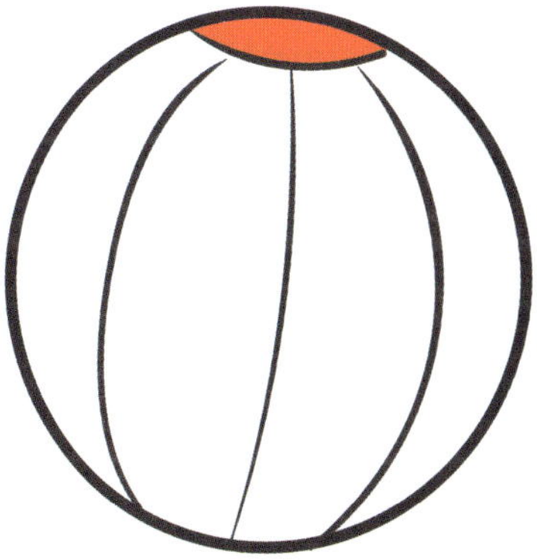

Color the ball **green**.

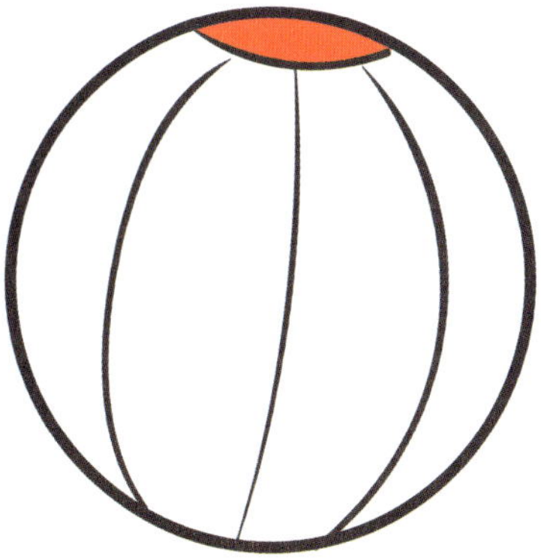

Color the ball **orange**.

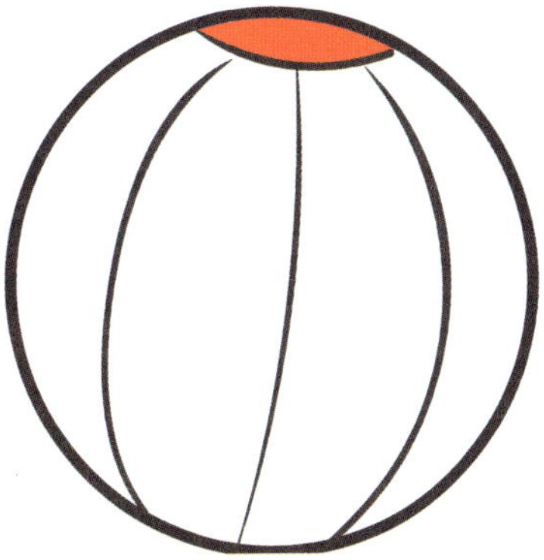

Color the ball **pink**.

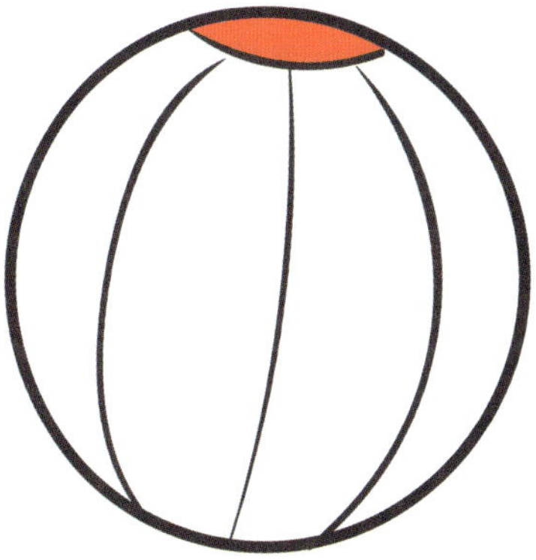

Color the ball **yellow**.

NUMBERS AND EARLY MATH

6, Six

Trace the number 6.

6 6 6 6 6 6

Draw **6** fish under the sea.

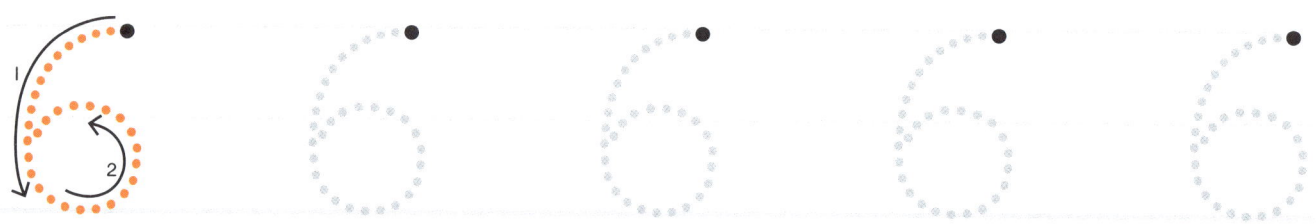

6 six

44

7, Seven

Trace the number **7**.

Draw a line to help Monkey find the box labelled **7**.

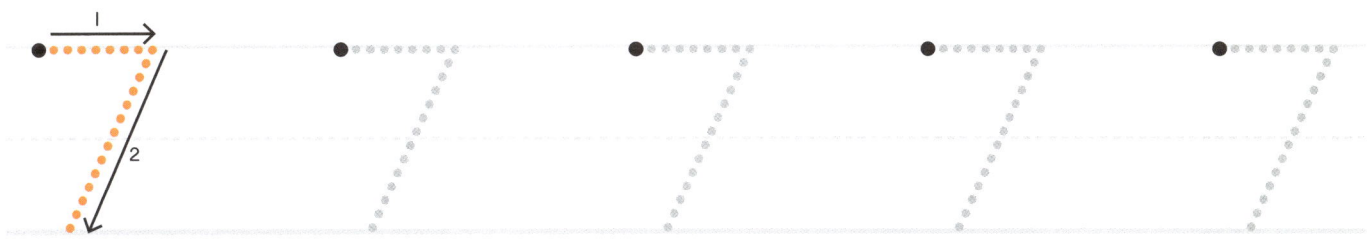

NUMBERS AND EARLY MATH

8, Eight

Trace the number 8.

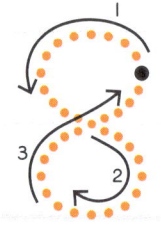    

Draw lines from the number 8 to the groups of 8.

eight

9, Nine

Trace the number 9.

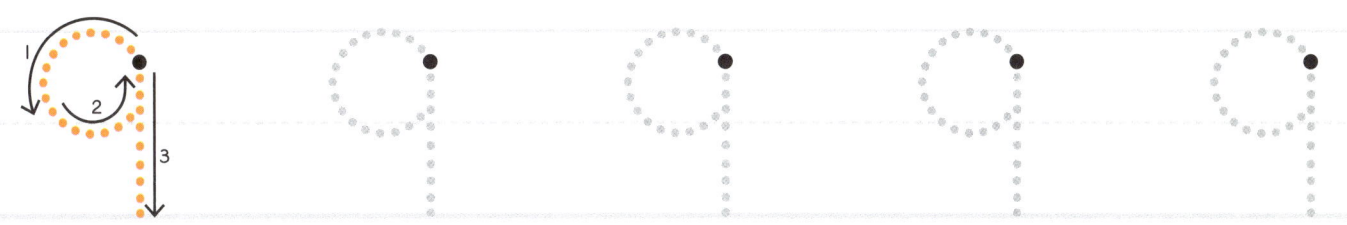

Circle 9 ice cream cones.

9 nine

NUMBERS AND EARLY MATH

10, Ten

Trace the number 10.

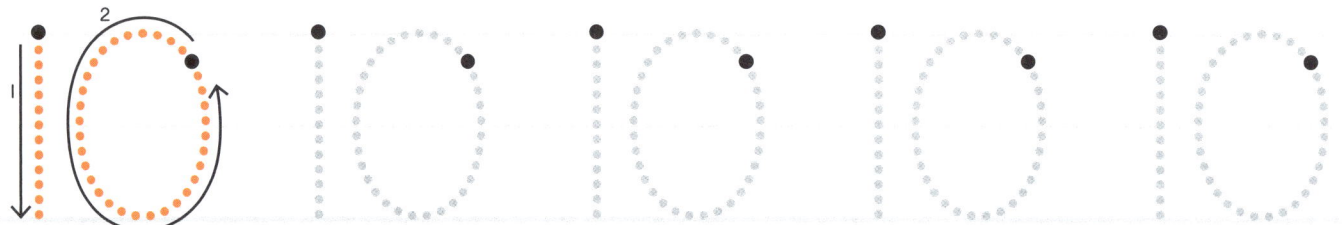

Trace along the path of green books to reach 10.

Numbers 0-10

Trace all of the **numbers** again.

0	1	2
zero	one	two
3	4	
three	four	
5	6	7
five	six	seven
8	9	10
eight	nine	ten

Great job learning your numbers!

49

NUMBERS AND EARLY MATH

Before

Trace the number that is **before** the other numbers. Use the example to help you.

one boat

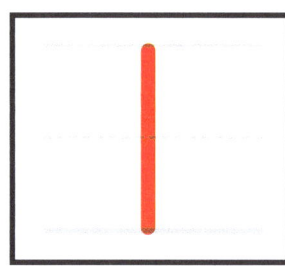 2 3

  3 4

 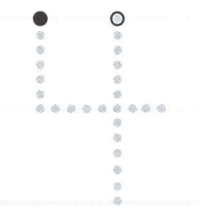 5 6

 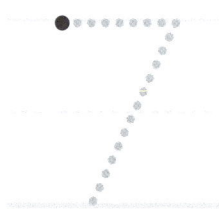 8 9

50

Between

Trace the number that is **between** the other numbers. Use the example to help you.

two party hats

1 \[2\] 3

3 4 5

5 6 7

8 9 10

NUMBERS AND EARLY MATH

After

Trace the number that is **after** the other numbers. Use the example to help you.

three bananas

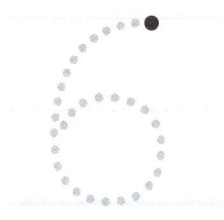

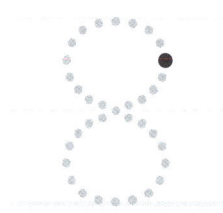 

Counting

Count the objects and **match** them to the correct number.

NUMBERS AND EARLY MATH

Comparing Amounts

Circle the picture that has the **same amount** as the first picture in each row.

More and Less

Count the objects and answer each question.

Circle the group that has **more**.

Circle the group that has **less**.

Circle the group that has **more**.

Circle the group that has **less**.

SORTING AND CLASSIFYING

Search and Find

Look at the key. **Find** and **circle** these objects on the page. Some appear more than once!

Key

boat

glove

pen

square

bag

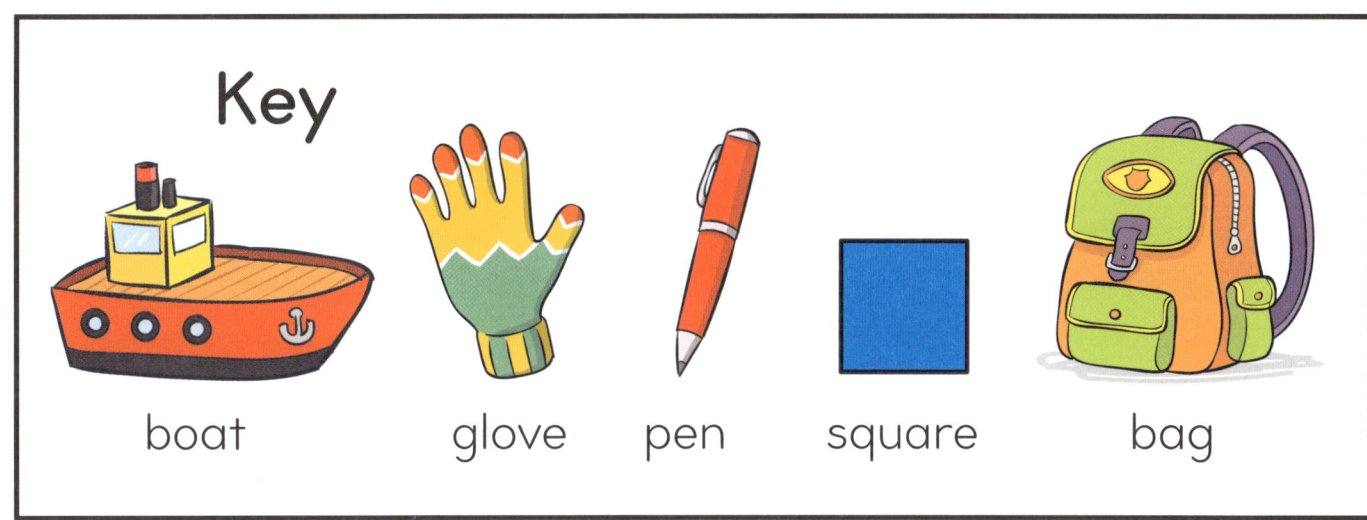

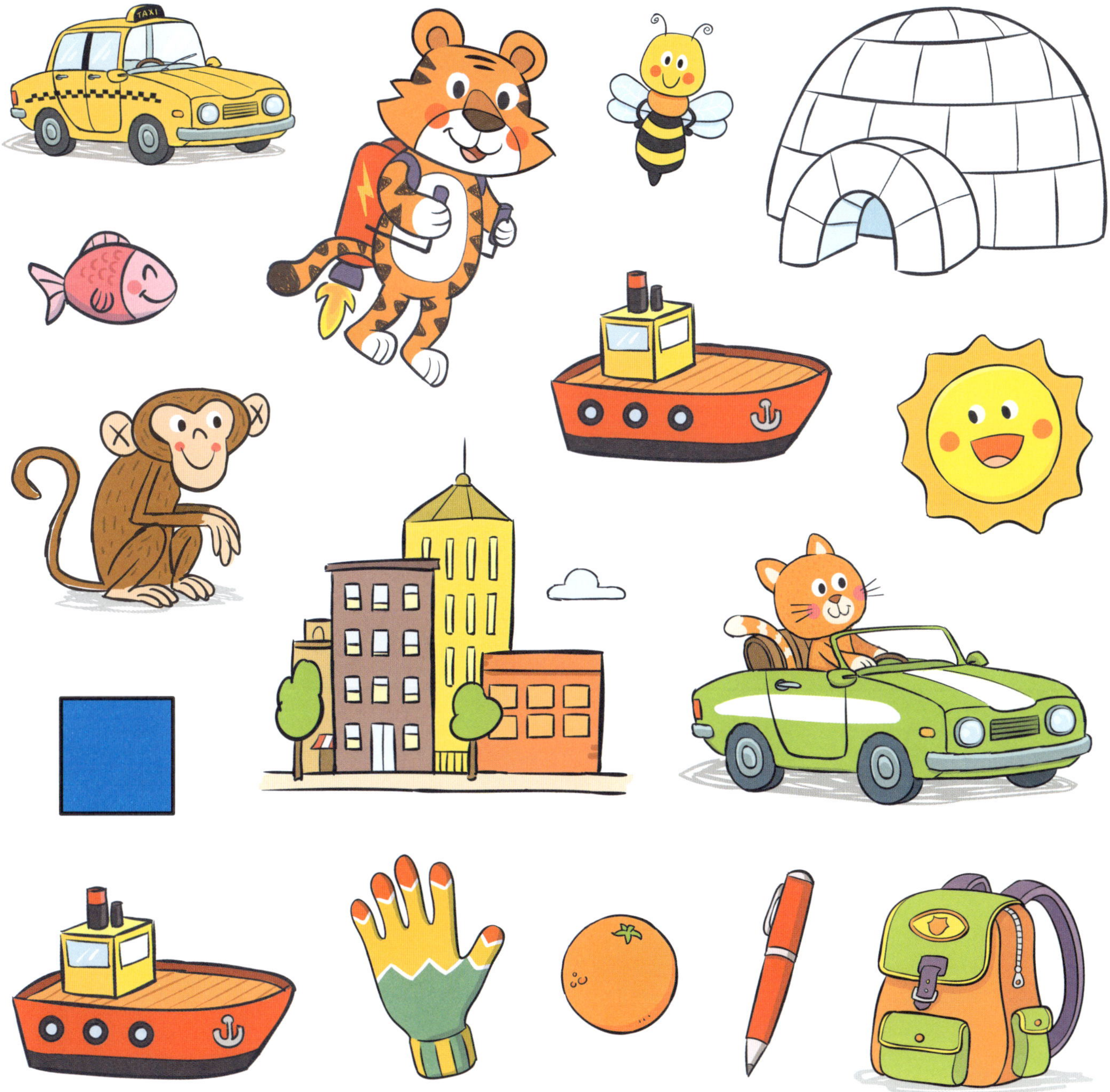

SORTING AND CLASSIFYING

Spot the Difference

Circle the picture that is **different** from the first one in each row.

SORTING AND CLASSIFYING

Comparing Size

Compare the animals and check the correct box.

Mouse is
☐ bigger ☐ smaller

Elephant is
☐ bigger ☐ smaller

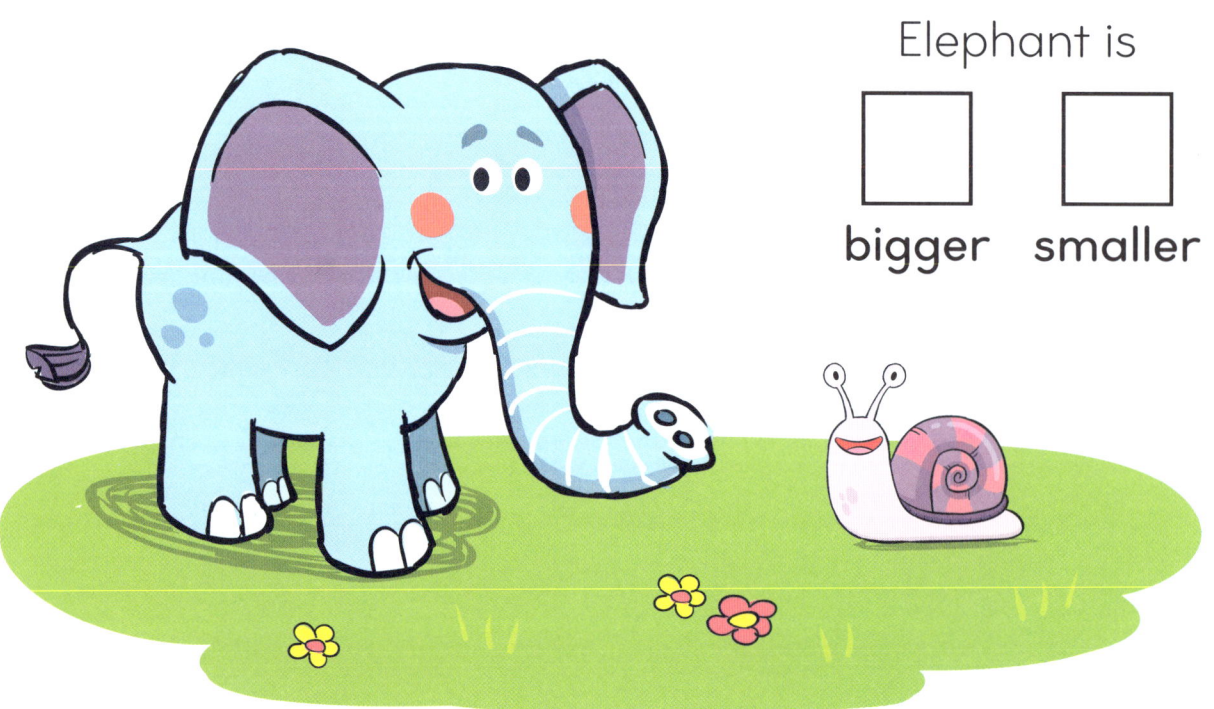

Positions

Let's learn about **positions**.

Circle the character at the **top**.

Circle the character at the **bottom**.

Circle the character in the **middle**.

SORTING AND CLASSIFYING

Pairs

Draw lines to **match** the **pairs** of characters.
Circle the character without a match.

Odd One Out

Cross out the picture in each row that does not belong with the others.

    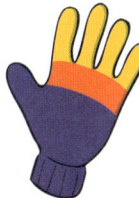

SORTING AND CLASSIFYING

Story Match

What happens next? Draw lines to match the **beginning** and the **end** of each story.

Beginning · End

Cub has a bun.

Yay! Thanks, Bee!

Oh no! My kite is stuck.

Yummy! All gone.

Beginning	End
 Let's visit the Snack Shack!	 Wheeee!
 Look! A slide!	 Great job!
 Let's go fishing!	 We love snacks!

OPPOSITES

Opposites

Draw lines to **match** the **opposites**.

little

cold

hot

down

up

big

happy

off

on

night

day

sad

EVERYDAY SKILLS

Day-to-Day

Starting with the example of **1**, write the numbers **2** through **6** to show the order of your daily routine.

  I take a bath.

  I eat lunch.

  I wake up.

  I go to bed.

  I go to school.

 I do homework.

Seasons

Summer, fall, winter, spring . . . which is your favorite season? Check your favorite.

☐ summer

☐ fall

☐ winter

☐ spring

EMOTIONS AND SENSES

Emotions

Draw lines to match the pictures to the **emotions**.

Senses

Draw lines to match the pictures to the **senses**.

BASIC VOCABULARY

Parts of the Body

Draw a line to match the label to the correct **body part**.

Food

Circle the **food** you like to eat!
Say the words out loud.

Animals

Draw lines to match the **animals** with the words.

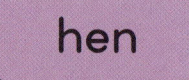

cat

dog

pig

fox

hen

frog

duck

fish

Following Instructions

Follow the **instructions** below.

1. Draw a ◯ around all the animals.
2. Draw a △ around the things you can eat.
3. Draw a ▢ around the things that go.

Answers

PENCIL CONTROL
Page 10:

Page 11:

COLORS
Page 12:
Match: the four colors to the correct four parts of the kite

Page 13:
Match: Octopus to purple;
orange to orange;
sun to yellow;
Pig to pink;
apple to red;
Dog to brown;
Frog to green;
book to blue

SHAPES
Page 15:
Color: circles in red; triangles in yellow; squares in blue; rectangles in green

ALPHABET
Page 22:
Match: A to a; B to b; C to c; D to d; E to e; F to f

Page 23:
Match: G to g; H to h; I to i; J to j; K to k; L to l; M to m

Page 24:
Match: N to n; O to o; P to p; Q to q; R to r; S to s

Page 25:
Match: T to t; U to u; V to v; W to w; X to x; Y to y; Z to z

Page 26:
Match: A to Ant; B to Bee; C to Cat; D to Dog; E to Elephant

Page 27:
Match: a to apple; b to book; c to carrot; d to dinosaur; e to eagle

Page 28:
Match: F to Frog; G to Goat; H to Hen; I to Iguana; J to Jaguar

Page 29:
Match: f to flower; g to grapes; h to hippo; i to igloo; j to jet

Page 30:
Match: K to Kangaroo; L to Lion; M to Mouse; N to Newt; O to Octopus

Page 31:
Match: k to kite; l to log; m to monkey; n to nest; o to orange

Page 32:
Match: P to Polar bear; Q to Quail; R to Rabbit; S to Snake; T to Tiger

Page 33:
Match: p to pig; q to queen; r to rainbow; s to snail; t to tent

Page 34:
U to Unicorn; V to Vulture; W to Walrus; X to X-ray fish; Y to Yeti; Z to Zebra

Page 35:
Match: u to umbrella; v to van; w to web; x to xylophone; y to yo-yo; z to zipper

Page 36:

Page 37:

NUMBERS AND EARLY MATH

Page 38:
There are **4** zeros to circle.

Page 39:
Color: **1** shape only

Page 40:
Draw lines to:
cats; **unicorns**

Page 41:
Circle: **3** apples

Page 42:
Circle: **Lion**

Page 43:
Color the **5** balls in the colors indicated.

Page 44:
Draw: **6** fish

Page 45:

Page 46:
Draw lines to:
beach balls; **pens**

Page 47:
Circle: **9** ice cream cones

Page 48:

Page 50:
2, 3, 4
4, 5, 6
7, 8, 9

Page 51:
3, **4**, 5
5, **6**, 7
8, **9**, 10

Page 52:
4, 5, **6**
6, 7, **8**
8, 9, **10**

Page 53:
Match: party hats to **2**; oranges to **6**; beach balls to **8**; boat to **1**; apples to **7**

Page 54:

Page 55:
Circle: **oranges**
Circle: **boat**
Circle: **apples**
Circle: **party hats**

SORTING AND CLASSIFYING

Pages 56-57:
Circle: **3** boats;
1 glove;
4 pens;
1 square;
2 bags

Page 58:

Page 59:

Page 60:
Mouse is **smaller**
Elephant is **bigger**

Page 61:
Circle: **Yeti**
Circle: **Bee**
Circle: **Alligator**

Page 62:
Match the pairs.
Elephant is the odd one out.

Page 63:
Yeti
Bag
Alligator
Jet

Pages 64-65:

OPPOSITES
Page 66:
Match:
little to **big**;
hot to **cold**;
up to **down**

Page 67:
Match:
happy to **sad**;
on to **off**;
day to **night**

EVERYDAY SKILLS
Page 68:
Suggested order:
I wake up;
I go to school;
I eat lunch;
I do homework;
I take a bath;
I go to bed

EMOTIONS AND SENSES
Page 70:
Match:
Beaver to **happy**;
Tiger to **sad**;
Crab to **angry**;
Dog to **worried**;
Bear to **surprised**

Page 71
Match:
Skunk to **smell**;
mice to **see**;
noodles to **taste**;
drums to **hear**;
bubble to **touch**

BASIC VOCABULARY
Page 72:
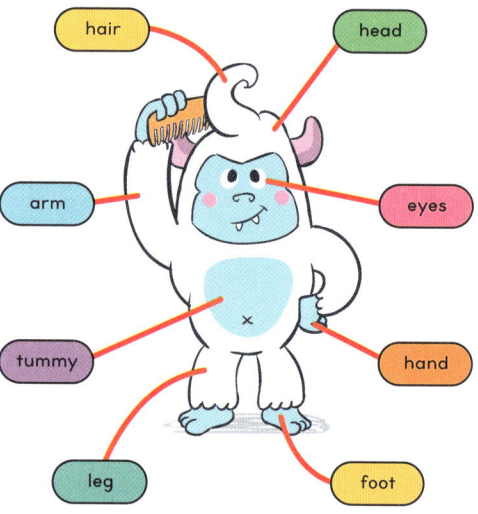

Page 74:

Page 75:
: **Frog**; **Pig**; **Cat**

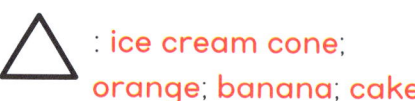: **ice cream cone**; **orange**; **banana**; **cake**

: **boat**; **jet**; **cab**; **truck**